HELP YOURSELF TO SAFETY

A Guide To Avoiding Dangerous Situations
With Strangers and Friends

by

Kate Hubbard

and

Evelyn Berlin

Foreword by

John and Revé Walsh

Illustrations by

Marina Megale

Edited by

Linda D. Meyer and

Carole Lyons

ROSLINDALE

The Chas. Franklin Press
18409-90th Avenue W., Edmonds, WA 98020

Dedication:
For Fanny Lowy and
Rose and Siggy

Acknowledgements:

The authors wish to thank the Adam Walsh Child Resource Center, Linda D. Meyer, and the members of our writer's group.
The publisher wishes to thank John and Brian Lee, Matt and Marci Erickson, Casey and Michael Doherty, Eric Raefield, Anthony Peters, Kim Jackson, and John and Revé Walsh.

THE CHILDREN'S SAFETY SERIES:
   PRIVATE ZONE: A Book Teaching Children Sexual Assault
      Prevention Tools by Frances S. Dayee
   SAFETY ZONE: A Book Teaching Child Abduction
      Prevention Tools by Linda D. Meyer
   HELP YOURSELF TO SAFETY: A Guide To Avoiding
      Dangerous Situations With Strangers and Friends
      by Kate Hubbard and Evelyn Berlin
   IT'S NOT YOUR FAULT by Judy Jance

ATTENTION: SCHOOLS AND ORGANIZATIONS

Our books are available at quantity discounts with bulk purchase for educational use. For information, please write to: Special Sales Dept., The Chas. Franklin Press, 18409 - 90th Ave. West, Edmonds, WA 98020.

Text copyright © 1985 by Kate Hubbard and Evelyn Berlin. Illustrations copyright © 1985 by Marina Megale. All rights reserved. This book, or parts thereof, may not be reproduced in any way, shape or form except for brief excerpts for review without the written permission of the publisher. ISBN 0-932091-00-8 (lib. bind.) ISBN 0-932091-01-6 (pap.) LCCN 84-082541. Printed in the United States of America.

FOREWORD

With the increased awareness and reporting of crimes against children, people are beginning to realize that the exploitation of children is a greater problem than was ever imagined. The abduction and sexual exploitation of children has always been America's hidden shame. We wanted to forget Atlanta. We wanted to forget Houston, to forget the Los Angeles school abuses. Now we are being forced to face them and to deal with them. They were never *NOT* there. They were just underreported, hidden behind closed doors and never brought to bear because the children had no voice.

People have to realize that this is a serious illness and phenomenon in this society, and they have to think of it as such and to treat it with prevention. This is 1984, not 1954. The old rules of society no longer exist.

It is estimated that 70% of molestation is done by someone the child knows in some way. This is a real problem because children are so trusting. They may fear a stranger, but are typically taught to trust someone they know.

The purpose of this book is to teach children prevention. We have always reacted *AFTER* the abuse of the child. We must educate our children to help themselves to safety *BEFORE* abuse takes place. We owe it to them to give them at least a 50-50 chance to make it to adulthood with no incident.

This education must be done in the schools as well as at home, because not all parents will choose to teach their children the concept of personal safety. We need education, awareness and prevention, concepts which are taught in HELP YOURSELF TO SAFETY.

America is a system of fifty feudal kingdoms called states. Very few of these states have seen fit to enfranchise children with rights. If you care about the quality of children's lives, *YOU* have to get involved in changing the laws of *YOUR* state. **PERMANENT CHANGES IN THE SYSTEM CAN BE ACCOMPLISHED ONLY THROUGH ACTS OF THE LEGISLATURE.***

We can no longer sit idle and pretend the problem doesn't exist, or will go away if only we ignore it long enough. It won't. If you care about the life and safety of your child, *GET INVOLVED.*

> John and Revé Walsh
> Adam Walsh Center,
> National Center for Missing
> and Exploited Children

* If you would like to know how to introduce laws into your state or how to lobby your congressman, write the National Center for Missing and Exploited Children or The Adam Walsh Center (Addresses at the back of the book.). Ask for the State Legislative Model of Children's Laws.

Why should your child read
HELP YOURSELF TO SAFETY?

With increasing frequency, reports of child-napping and molestation send shock waves through communities of all sizes and all ethnic and social backgrounds. These crimes are not limited to isolated areas. They are happening across the country. No matter where they live, boys and girls of all ages are potentially at risk.

Statistics on child molestation vary enormously. The conservative estimates now generally accepted are that 1 in 4 girls and 1 in 6 boys will be sexually molested in some way by age 18. Eighty-five percent of the time it will be by someone the child knows.

Many young victims don't step forward because they feel they are to blame and are too ashamed to ask for help. Others are terrified of the possible negative repercussions should they reveal their secret. Nobody knows how many children have tried to escape their situations by telling about it, only to be accused of lying.

Child molesters come from all walks of life. Many were abused themselves as children. They are men and women of all ages. Most are well-known to their victims — they may be acquaintances, friends, teachers or daycare providers — even relatives. What makes child molesters so dangerous is that most do not stop at one assault, or one victim. The victimizing of a particular child may go on for months or years, and when that child becomes unavailable or unattractive, the molester will usually turn to another. Reports of people abusing 60 or 70 children apiece are not uncommon.

Child molesters claim they love their victims, and in most cases they do not brutalize the children. On the other hand, strangers who abduct children are often child-haters. These people pose the greatest threat to children. One hundred fifty thousand American children are abducted each year, 100,000 by the non-custodial parent, and 50,000 by strangers.

For your child to be protected against molestation and abduction, he/she needs to know (1) that these things can happen, (2) how to recognize dangerous situations with strangers and people he/she knows, and (3) how to handle these situations. HELP YOURSELF TO SAFETY assists children in learning this information. It shows them how to take responsibility for their own actions and how to minimize the risks of danger. This book is meant as a starting point to ongoing discussions about personal safety. We encourage you to go over the safety rules at the back of the book, not once but many times. **ONCE IS NOT ENOUGH!** If adults keep the channels of communication open, children are more likely to know they can reveal anything that has happened in the past and tell about anything that may happen in the future.

Evelyn Berlin

Kate Hubbard

HELP YOURSELF TO SAFETY

You are growing up. You go to school. You visit friends. You go places by yourself.

Your parents can't watch out for you when you are alone. They can't protect you from

someone who may want to hurt you or take you away.

What can you do?

<u>You</u> can learn to keep <u>yourself</u> safe. The children in this book will show you how.

Peter is afraid to walk to school. Every day he walks down an alley. He passes a street corner where big kids hang out. Sometimes these kids tease him. Peter goes through a park

where street people sleep on the benches and nice-looking strangers often speak to him.

Peter is tired of being afraid. What will he do?

Peter asks his parents for help. Together, they check out his neighborhood. They find a safer route for him to follow. Peter's parents show him houses where they know the people. They show him stores that are good places to run to if he needs help.

Now, Peter is not afraid to walk to school.

Ask your mom or dad to help you check out your neighborhood. Find out where it is safest for you to walk. When you go to and from school, stay with other kids. Walking in a group is safer than walking alone.

"I hate rain," says Molly.

Just then, a car zooms past. It splashes muddy water all over her favorite book bag — the one with her name on it.

"Oh no," she cries. "What a mess!"

Another car pulls up next to Molly and stops. The driver is a man she doesn't know. He rolls down the window.

"Hi, Molly!" he calls out. "Your father said I should give you a ride to school."

Should Molly get into the car?

Molly hesitates. She's never seen the man before. 'Does he really know my father?' she wonders. 'How does he know my name?'

"I don't know you," says Molly. "I won't go with you unless you tell me the code word."

"Your father forgot to tell me the code word," says the man. "But it's okay. He knows me."

"Well, I don't," says Molly. "I won't go with you." As she clutches the book bag to her chest, Molly realizes how the man knew her name. He saw it printed on the bag!

'This man is trying to trick me," Molly thinks. 'He might want to hurt me or take me away.'

Molly turns and runs away as fast as she can. She doesn't stop until she reaches a place her parents have told her is safe. She tells an adult there what happened.

Did Molly do the right thing? Yes. She did exactly the right thing.

If your name is on your hat, knapsack, or shirt, wear it only at home. If a stranger wants to hurt you, knowing your name makes it easier for him or her to trick you.

Never go away with anyone you don't know, even if the person seems very nice. Not all people are nice. Some people hurt children.

Set up a code word with your parents. A code word is a special word that you and your parents agree on. No one else knows it. It is used only in emergencies. If someone has to pick you up, your parents tell him the code word. When you hear your code word, you know it is safe to go with that person.

Todd goes into the restroom at the library. Standing by the toilet is an older boy. The boy leans against the wall and watches Todd.

The older boy makes Todd feel uncomfortable. Todd worries that the boy might want to touch his private parts or rob him of his money.

Should Todd stay in the restroom?

Todd turns around and walks out. He waits until he sees the boy leave. Then he asks a friend to go into the restroom with him.

When you need to use a public restroom, ask someone you know to go with you. Never stay in any restroom if someone there makes you feel uncomfortable. When no one else is near, strangers sometimes harm children in public buildings. For this reason, you also need to be alert when you go into places like elevators, hallways, and restrooms by yourself.

If a stranger attacks you, run and yell "Help! He's hurting me!" If you can't get away, bite, kick, and scratch the person. Keep on shouting for help.

Jessica is home alone. She is watching TV while she waits for her parents to come home from work. The door bell rings.

Should Jessica answer the door?

Jessica knows that people sometimes try to trick children when they are home alone. The person on the other side of the door might want to harm Jessica. Instead of answering the door, she goes to the phone and waits. If the person tries to break in, Jessica is ready to call the police.

When you are home alone, **never answer the door.** Keep the numbers of the police and of a neighbor you trust near your phone. Don't be afraid to call them if you think someone is trying to break into your house.

Becky likes to play with her babysitter. With the blocks, they build towers. With the puppets, they perform plays. With the medical kit, they play doctor.

"I have a great idea," says the babysitter. "If you take off your clothes for me now, I'll make popcorn for you later."

What should Becky do?

Becky knows that her body is private. No one has the right to look at it or touch it without her permission.

Becky is scared, but she says, "No way! I'm not allowed to do that. I'm going to watch television instead."

When her parents return, Becky tells them what happened.

Did Becky handle this well? Yes, she did.

If someone you know tries to look at or touch your private parts, you have the right to say "no." **Your body belongs to you. No one has the right to touch it without your permission.** If someone asks you to look at or touch their body, you may say "no," too. Tell your parents about any requests that make you feel uneasy.

Sometimes, your doctor needs to check your private parts to be sure you are all right. But, even the doctor has to have a good reason to touch you. If it makes you uncomfortable, talk it over with your parents.

Aaron and his friends walk by a construction site where new homes are being built.

"Look, nobody's there!" says one of the boys. "Now's our chance to check it out.

"That's not such a great idea," says Aaron. "We're not supposed to play there."

"What's the matter, Aaron? Are you chicken?" replies the boy.

Should Aaron go along with his friends?

"No!" says Aaron, indignantly. "I'm not chicken. I'm smart. Somebody could get hurt down there. I don't want it to be me."

"We'll see you later, Scaredy-cat," says another one of the boys. "You're sure going to miss a good time."

"That's okay," says Aaron. "I don't mind. I'll be sure to send you guys flowers when you land in the hospital."

Sometimes your friends might want you to do things that are dangerous or against the law. It isn't easy to say "no" but often it's the smartest thing to do. Think up some answers ahead of time and practice them. Then, if someone asks you to do something you know you shouldn't, you'll have an answer handy. Here are some lines you can use:

I'll send flowers to your funeral.
I'll visit you in jail.
I'll stop by to see you in the hospital.

Scott stops to look at toys while shopping with his mom. He finds a battery-powered robot that he wants to show her. He looks up and down the aisle but doesn't see her.

"Mom!" yells Scott. "Where are you?"

His mother doesn't answer. She is gone! What should Scott do?

Scott sees a cash register. He runs over to the sales clerk standing behind it. "I've lost my mom," says Scott.

The sales clerk pages his mother over the loudspeaker. She soon appears and gives Scott a big hug.

When you go shopping with your parents, always keep an eye on them. If you wander off, they can't see or hear you. If a stranger tried to take you away, your parents wouldn't be able to help you. Remember, not all people are nice.

If you do get lost, look for a sales clerk at a cash register, or a mom with little kids. These people are the ones most likely to help you.

All the children in this book learned to be alert. Being aware of what's going on around them helps keep them safe.

If you stay alert and aware, you can help yourself to safety, too. Notice the people and things around you. Learn what to do in

dangerous situations. Trust your feelings! If someone or something makes you feel afraid, it's okay to run away. You are important to your family and your friends. You need to keep yourself safe for them, as well as for yourself.

SAFETY TIPS FOR ADULTS

1. Make sure your child realizes it is almost impossible to tell by appearances which strangers may try to hurt him. Dangerous strangers may be young or old, male or female, good-looking or homely, and of any race.
2. A potential abductor may try to make a child feel sorry for him or want to help him. Tell your child that no matter what a person says, the child should never go with anyone unless you have given the child permission or the person gives the correct code word.
3. Be aware that the most-likely places for child abductions are fairs, carnivals, shopping malls, and public restrooms.
4. Never leave a child alone in a car.
5. Do not allow your child's picture and name to appear together in the newspaper.
6. Show your child the homes and shops in your neighborhood that are safe places to seek help in case of danger.
7. Tell your child where to go if he needs help and you are not home. Clear this arrangement ahead of time with the person you want your child to go to.
8. If your child walks to school or if you leave home before your child boards the school bus, arrange with the school's principal to have someone notify you when your child is absent.
9. If you are a divorced parent and are afraid that your former spouse might kidnap your child, ask a lawyer about supervised visitation.
10. Keep up-to-date photographs of your child available in case he is abducted.
11. If a child is reluctant, do not force him to hug or kiss relatives or friends. Back up your child's right to say NO to a request for touch that is not wanted.
12. Admit to your child when you are wrong about something. This shows your child that adults are not always right.
13. Discuss the differences between secrets and surprises with your children. Everyone finds out about surprises in the end. Secrets hide things. They are used by child molesters to keep people from discovering what is going on.
14. If your child tells you he does not want to go with or be with someone — listen. There could be a reason.
15. If your child chooses an adult for a best friend instead of another child, find out what is going on between them.
16. If your child tells you he has been sexually abused, believe him. Children do not lie about this.
17. Change your "code word" once it has been used.

SAFETY TIPS FOR CHILDREN

1. Never go with anyone you don't know. If someone tries to grab you, scream "HE'S HURTING ME!" Try to run away. Kick and hit as hard as you can.
2. Never leave school with anyone unless it has been arranged ahead of time or the person tells you the correct code word.
3. If an adult asks you for help or directions, say, "I CAN'T HELP YOU." It may sound rude, but it's the safe thing to do. Adults should ask other adults for help. They should not ask children.
4. If you get separated from your parent while shopping, go immediately to the nearest sales clerk and ask for help.
5. Don't advertise your name by wearing clothing or carrying a bookbag with your name on it.
6. Never go into someone else's house without first telling your parent.
7. Whenever possible, walk in a group, not alone.
8. When you are home alone, don't answer the door or tell anyone over the phone that you are by yourself.
9. Know your address and phone number, including the area code.
10. Learn how to make a long distance collect call. If you get scared when you are away from home, you can call your parent without asking permission.
11. Learn to say NO to friends.
12. You have the right to say NO to anyone who wants to touch you, or who wants you to touch them.
13. Trust your feelings. If someone says or does anything that makes you uncomfortable, tell your parent.
14. Tell a parent if an adult or older child asks you to keep a secret. Secrets are okay between children of the same age, but often secrets between an older person and a child are used to hide things that your parents should know.
15. Tell a parent if anyone tries to photograph you.

The "What if ...?" Game

For most children, the ability to generalize does not develop until they reach their early teenage years. Without this ability, children cannot apply the lessons learned from one situation to another similar one. Therefore, it is important to discuss with children how to respond in a responsible manner to a wide variety of dangerous or potentially dangerous situations.

Pose each of the following situations to your child. Discuss the best response. Make up additional scenarios of your own and discuss them, too. This doesn't need to be work. Make it into a game.

What would you do if:

1. A nice-looking man gives you quarters to play video games and then asks you to pose for pictures in return.
2. A well-dressed woman tells you that you have the right face to become a model and offers you a high-paying job.
3. An older woman using a cane asks you to carry her groceries into her apartment.
4. A clown on the playground offers you popcorn.
5. On a bus, a grandmotherly-looking woman takes the seat beside you. She talks in a pleasant way and then begins to grope around your lap with her hand.
6. A small pick-up truck pulls up next to you as you are walking down the street. The driver asks you for directions.
7. At a carnival, a well-dressed man offers to buy you food or a ticket for your favorite ride.
8. A tearful middle-aged woman tells you she has lost a kitten or puppy and asks you to help her find it.
9. A man approaches you near your school and tells you his daughter is in the sixth grade there. He says she was supposed to meet him but didn't. He wants you to help him find her classroom.
10. Someone standing close to you on a crowded bus starts to touch your private parts.
11. A businessman shows you pictures of children who have no clothes on.
12. A person who appears to be a police officer flashes a badge at you. He says he has been informed that you are carrying matches. He wants to search you.
13. The janitor at school tells you he'll give you money if you stay after school and if you can keep a secret.
14. Your neighbor comes to pick you up at school. He says your mother is hurt but he doesn't know your code word.
15. An older child in your neighborhood shows you his or her private parts.
16. You are babysitting and the husband and wife have gone out separately. The husband returns first and tells you he can't take you home until his wife arrives because he can't leave the kids alone.
17. You are sitting in your uncle's lap and he begins to touch you in a way that makes you feel uncomfortable.
18. You are with your friend and his or her parents. They tell you and your friend to stay in the car while they go into a store or a shopping mall.
19. Your friend's parents aren't home, but your friend wants you to come over anyway.

20. Your friend offers you some pills and says they will make you feel great.
21. While shopping, your friend asks you to take some candy, put it in your pocket, and walk out of the store without paying for it.

Now think about the following situations. As a parent, how would you react if these or similar situations arose?
1. A friendly neighbor frequently offers to take neighborhood children deep-sea fishing, camping and on other exciting excursions.
2. It has been rumored that the minister of your church, whom you respect, has been molesting children in the youth group.
3. On the beach or when you are shopping, a stranger strikes up a conversation with your child.
4. Your child tells you that Grandpa tried to touch his or her private parts.
5. The teller in the bank offers your child a lollipop, or the clerk in the bakery offers your child a cookie.
6. Your child's daycare provider doesn't want parents to pick up children early and is reluctant to have you stay long when you drop off your child. She claims it disrupts her routine.
7. The doctor asks you to leave the room while your child is being examined.
8. Your father or mother insists on kissing your child when the child doesn't want to be touched.

RESOURCES: Books For Children.

Prices subject to change without prior notice. Generally, add $1.00 for shipping and handling.

SAFETY ZONE: A Book Teaching Children Abduction Prevention Skills by Linda D. Meyer; illustrations by Marina Megale; The Charles Franklin Press, 18409 90th Ave. W. Edmonds, WA 98020; 1984; $3.00; ages 3-11.

PRIVATE ZONE: A Book Teaching Children Sexual Assault Prevention Tools by Frances S. Dayee, illustrations by Marina Megale; Warner Books; 1982; $2.95; ages 3-9.

THE DANGERS OF STRANGERS by Carole G. Vogel and Kathryn A. Goldner; illustrations by Lynette Schmidt; Dillon Press, Inc., 242 Portland Avenue South, Minneapolis, MN 55415; 1983; $10.95; ages 4-9.

IT'S MY BODY: A Book To Teach Young Children How To Resist Uncomfortable Touch by Lory Freeman; illustrations by Carol Deach; Parenting Press, 7750-31st Ave. NE, Seattle, WA 98115; 1982; $3.00; ages 2-6.

NO MORE SECRETS FOR ME by Oralee Wachter; illustrations by Jane Aaron; Little Brown and Co.; 1983; $4.95; ages 6-10.

ONCE I WAS A LITTLE BIT FRIGHTENED by J. Williams; Rape and Abuse Crisis Center of Fargo-Moorhead, Fargo, North Dakota; 1980; ages 5-10.

WHAT IF I SAY NO!! by Jill Haddad and Lloyd Martin, M.H. Cap & Co., PO Box 3584, Bakersfield, CA 93385; ages 3-12. $3.50

MY VERY OWN SPECIAL BODY BOOK by Kerry Bassett, Hawthorne Press; 1980; $3.95; preschool.

PLAY IT SAFE: The Kid's Guide To Personal Safety And Crime Prevention by Kathy S. Kyte; Knopf; 1983; $5.95; ages 6-teen.

ALL ALONE AFTER SCHOOL by Muriel Stanek; Albert Whitman; 1984; $9.25; ages 6-9.

WHO IS A STRANGER AND WHAT SHOULD I DO? by Linda Walvoord Girard; Albert Whitman; 1984; $9.25; ages 7-11.

MY BODY IS PRIVATE by Linda Walvoord Girard; Albert Whitman; 1984; $9.25; ages 4-8.

FEELING SAFE, FEELING STRONG: How to Avoid Sexual Abuse and What to Do If It Happens to You by Susan N. Terkel and Janice E. Rench; Lerner; 1984; $9.95; ages 9-13.

SEXUAL ABUSE: Let's Talk About It by Margaret O. Hyde; The Westminster Press; 1984; $10.95; ages 10-up.

ON MY OWN: The Kids' Self Care Book by Lynette Long, Ph.D.; Acropolis Books LTD; 1984; $7.95.

MY VERY OWN BOOK ABOUT ME by Jo Stowell and Mary Dietzel; Spokane Rape Crisis Center, Lutheran Social Services, N. 1226 Howard, Spokane, WA 99201; 1980; $2.00.

RESOURCES: Books For Adults

Prices subject to change without prior notice. Generally, add $1.00 for shipping and handling.

THE SILENT CHILDREN: A Book for Parents About the Prevention of Child Abuse by Linda Tschirhart Sanford; Anchor Press/Doubleday; 1980; $7.95.

CHILD LURES: A Guide to Prevent Abduction by Ken Wooden; Ralston Purina Company, Breakfast Foods Division, Checkerboard Square, St. Louis, MO 63164; 1984; $1.00.

HE TOLD ME NOT TO TELL by King County Rape Relief; King County Rape Relief, 305 South 43rd Avenue, Renton, WA 98055; 1979; WE HAVE A SECRET by Lloyd Martin and Jill Haddad; M. H. Cap & Company, P.O. Box 3584, Bakersfield, CA 93385; 1982; $12.50.

PROTECT YOUR CHILD FROM SEXUAL ABUSE: A Parent's Guide by Janie Hart-Rossi; Parenting Press Inc., Suite 412, 7750 31st Avenue North East, Seattle, WA 98115; 1984; $5.00.

NO MORE SECRETS: Protecting Your Child from Sexual Assault by Caren Adams and Jennifer Fay; Impact Publishers, P.O. Box 1094, San Luis Obispo, CA 93406; 1981; $3.95.

PUBLIC CONCERN AND PERSONAL ACTION: Sexual Child Abuse and A MESSAGE TO PARENTS ABOUT: Child Sexual Abuse by Children's Hospital National Medical Center; Child Protection Center/Special Unit, Children's Hospital National Medical Center, 111 Michigan Avenue NW, Washington, D.C. 20010; 1980; for a contribution.

HOW TO RAISE A STREET SMART CHILD: The Complete Parent's Guide to Safety on the Street and at Home, by Grace Hechinger; Facts on File; 1984; $14.95.

CHILD SNATCHING: How to Prevent It From Happening to Your Child by Michael W. Schaeffer; McGraw-Hill; 1984; $6.95.

JENNY'S NEW GAME by Laurella Cross; Eastwood Printing, P.O. Box 2933, Roswell, NM 88201; 1984; $8.95.

THE COMMON SECRET: Sexual Abuse of Children and Adolescents by Ruth S. and Henry Kemp; W. H. Freeman; 1984; $7.95.

YOUR CHILDREN SHOULD KNOW by Flora Colao and Tamar Hosansky; Bobbs-Merrill; 1983; $16.95.

THE BEST KEPT SECRET: Sexual Abuse of Children by Florence Rush; Prentice-Hall; 1980; $11.95.

HIDDEN VICTIMS: The Sexual Abuse of Children by Robert L. Geiser; Beacon Press; 1979.

MEN WHO RAPE: The Psychology of the Offender by A. Nichols Groth; Plenum Press; 1979.

KISS DADDY GOODNIGHT: A Speakout on Incest by Louise Armstrong; Hawthorne Books; 1978.

CONSPIRACY OF SILENCE: The Trauma of Incest by Sandra Butler; New Glide Publications; 1978.

BETRAYAL OF INNOCENCE: Incest and Its Devastation by Susan Forward and Craig Buck; Penguin Books; 1978.

SEXUALLY VICTIMIZED CHILDREN by David Finkelhor; Free Press; 1979.

CHILDREN IN THE CROSSFIRE: The Tragedy of Parental Kidnapping by Sally Abrahms; Atheneum; 1983.

KYLES' STORY: Friday Never Came: The Search For Missing People by John D. Clinkscales; Vantage; 1981.

PARENTAL CHILD-STEALING by Michael W. Agopian; Lexington Books; 1981.

STOLEN CHILDREN by John Edward Gill; Seaview Books; 1981.

STRATEGIES FOR FREE CHILDREN: A Guide to Child Assault Prevention by Sally Cooper; CAP, Box 02084, Columbus, OH 43202; $20.00.

RESOURCES: Audiovisual Materials.

Contact the following for brochures about their materials.

BUBBYLONIAN ENCOUNTER: A Play for Children About the Sense of Touch; Bubbylonian Productions; 1980; Kansas Committee for the Prevention of Child Abuse, 214 West 6th Street, Suite 301, Topeka, KS 66603.

CHILD MOLESTATION — WHEN TO SAY NO; AIMS Instructional Media, Inc., 626 Justin Avenue, Glendale, CA 91201; 1978.

BOYS BEWARE; AIMS Instructional Media, Inc., 626 Justin Avenue, Glendale, CA 91201.

GIRLS BEWARE; AIMS Instructional Media, Inc., 626 Justin Avenue, Glendale, CA 91201.

TOUCH CONTINUUM; Illusion Theatre, 528 Hennipin Avenue No. 309, Minneapolis, MN 55403; 1980.

WHO DO YOU TELL?; MTI Teleprograms, Inc., 3710 Commercial Avenue, Northbrook, IL 60062; ages 7-12.

HANDS OFF BILL; M. H. Cap and Company, P.O. Box 3584, Bakersfield, CA 93385.

TALKING ABOUT TOUCHING WITH PRESCHOOLERS; Committee for Children, P.O. Box 51049, Seattle, WA 98115; 1983.

SOME SECRETS SHOULD BE TOLD; Family Information Systems, 69 Clinton Road, Brookline, MA 02146; 1982; young children.

CHILD SAFE PRODUCTS CATALOG; Child Safe Products, Inc., 449 North University Drive, Plantation, FL 33324; ages 5-13.

YOU'RE IN CHARGE: You're in Charge, Inc. 1618 Yale Avenue, Salt Lake City, UT 84105; 1978.

For listing of other audiovisual materials, contact: Film Fair Communications, 10900 Ventura Blvd., P.O. Box 1728, Studio City, CA 91604.

RESOURCES: Organizations.

The National Child Abuse Hotline — Referral Service 1-(800)-422-4453.

1. Child Find, Inc.
   7 Innes Avenue
   Post Office Box 277
   New Paltz, New York 12561
   (914) 255-1848

2. National Center for Missing and Exploited Children
   1835 K Street N.W. Suite 700
   Washington, D.C. 20006
   (202) 634-9821

3. Adam Walsh Child Resource Center, Inc.
   1876 North University Drive, Suite 306
   Fort Lauderdale, FL 33322
   (305) 475-4847

4. Dee Scofield Awareness Program
   4418 Bay Court Avenue
   Tampa, FL 33611
   (813) 839-5025

5. North Dakota Rape and Abuse Crisis Center
   P.O. Box 1655
   Fargo, North Dakota 58107
   (701) 293-7273

6. Society for Young Victims
   29 Thurston Avenue
   Newport, RI 02840
   (401) 847-5083

7. Abducted Children's Rights of Canada
   P.O. Box 262, Station M
   Toronto, Ontario M6S 4T3
   (416) 498-5835

8. The Tonia Murrell Missing Children's Society
   9913 151st Street
   Edmonton, Alberta T5P 1T2
   (403) 486-7777

RESOURCES: Workshops/Curriculum

The following resources offer excellent programs to teach child personal safety. Please contact them for detailed information.

1. S.A.F.E.
   541 Avenue of The Americas
   New York, NY 10011
   (212) 242-4874

2. T.I.P.S.
   Jefferson Bldg.
   Fourth Street NW
   Charlottesville, VA 22901

3. Committee For Children
   PO Box 51049
   Seattle, WA 98115
   (206) 522-5834

4. Survival Skills For Children
   18509 85th Ave. West
   Edmonds, WA 98020
   (206) 778-9368

30